Kids Can Draw
DINOSAURS

by Philippe Legendre

Walter Foster

Attention Parents and Teachers

All children can draw a circle, a square, or a triangle…which means that they can also learn to draw a dimetrodon, triceratops, or pterodactyl! The KIDS CAN DRAW learning method is easy and fun. Children will learn a technique and a vocabulary of shapes that will form the basis for all kinds of drawing.

Pictures are created by combining geometric shapes to form a mass of volumes and surfaces. From this stage, children can give character to their sketches with straight, curved, or broken lines.

With just a few strokes of the pencil, a dinosaur will appear—and with the addition of color, the picture will be real work of art!

The KIDS CAN DRAW method offers a real apprenticeship in technique and a first look at composition, proportion, shapes, and lines. The simplicity of this method ensures that the pleasure of drawing is always the most important factor.

About Philippe Legendre

French painter, engraver, and illustrator, Philippe Legendre also runs a school of art for children aged 6–14 years. Legendre frequently spends time in schools and has developed this method of learning so that all children can discover the artist within themselves.

Helpful Tips

1. Each picture is made up of simple geometric shapes, which are illustrated at the top of the left-hand page. This is called the **Vocabulary of Shapes.** Encourage children to practice drawing each shape before starting their pictures.

2. Suggest children use a pencil to do their sketches. This way, if they don't like a particular shape, they can just erase it and try again.

3. A dotted line indicates that the line should be erased. Have children draw the whole shape and then erase the dotted part of the line.

4. Once children finish their drawings, they can color them with crayons, colored pencils, or felt-tip markers. They may want to go over the lines with a black pencil or pen.

Now let's get started!

The iguanodon…

has big square teeth,

but don't be scared—

she just eats leaves.

Iguanodon

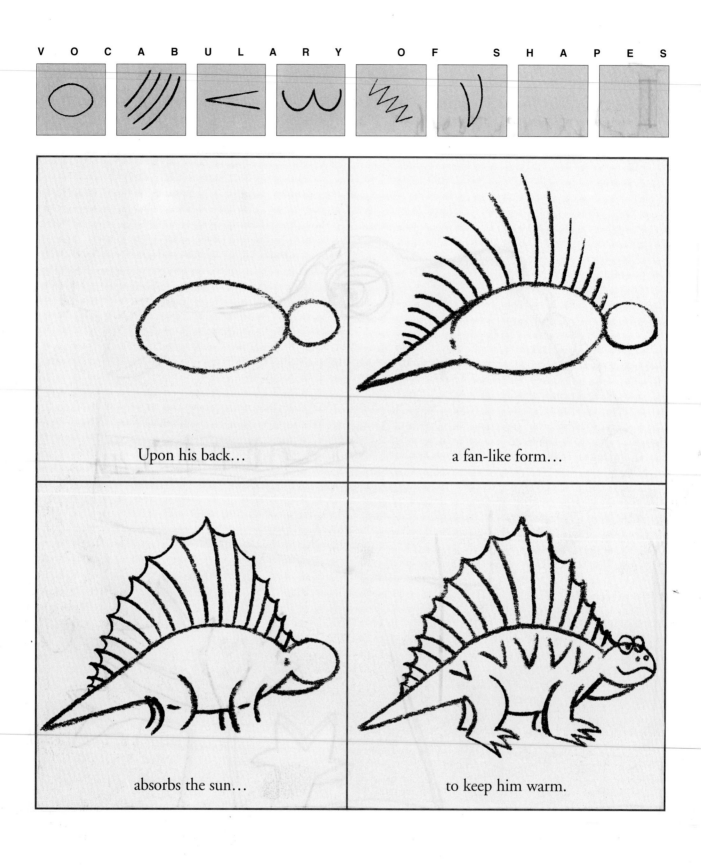

Upon his back…

a fan-like form…

absorbs the sun…

to keep him warm.

Dimetrodon

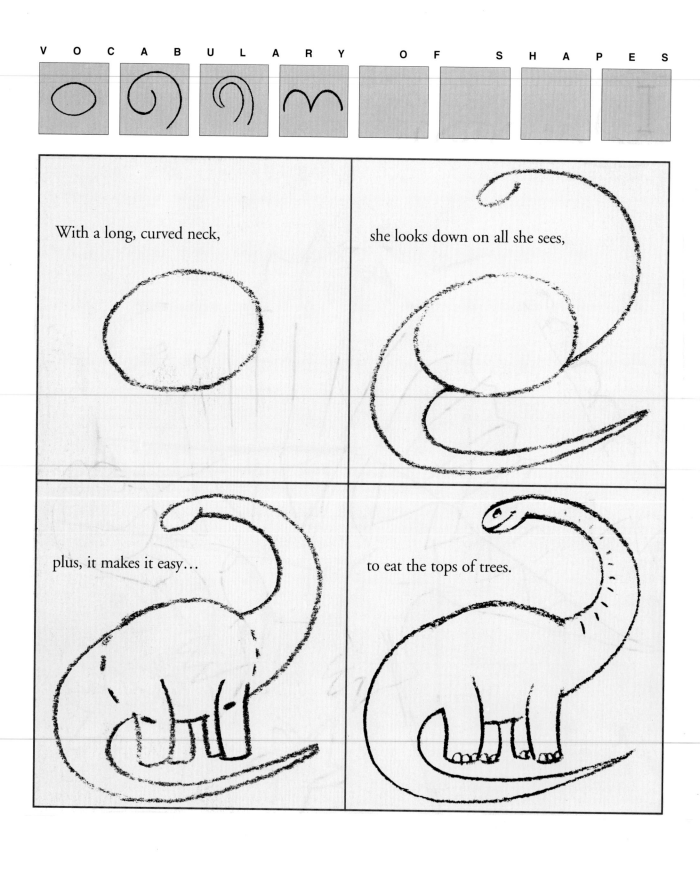

With a long, curved neck,

she looks down on all she sees,

plus, it makes it easy…

to eat the tops of trees.

Diplodocus

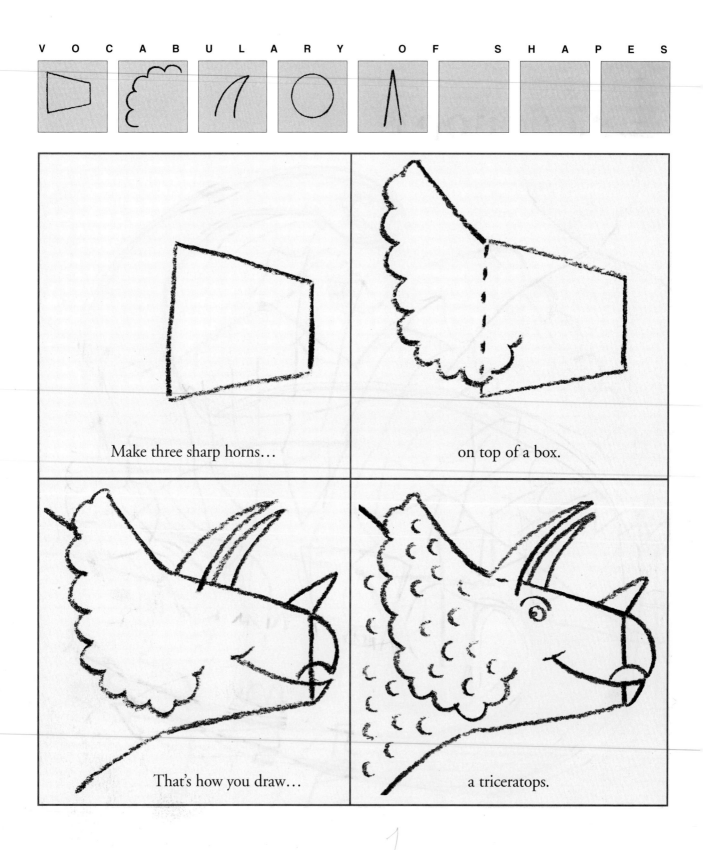

Make three sharp horns…

on top of a box.

That's how you draw…

a triceratops.

Triceratops

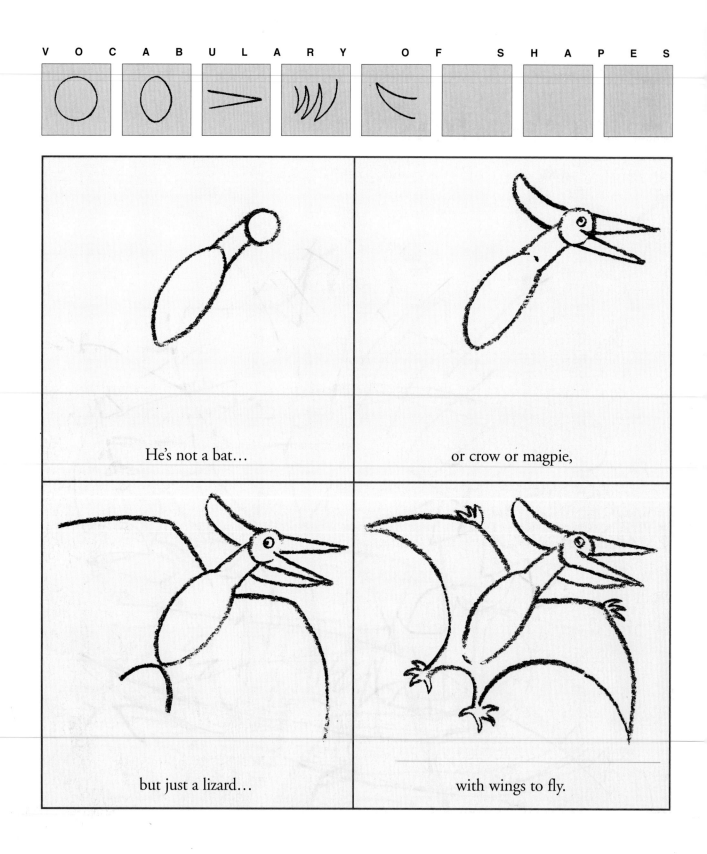

He's not a bat...

or crow or magpie,

but just a lizard...

with wings to fly.

Pteranodon

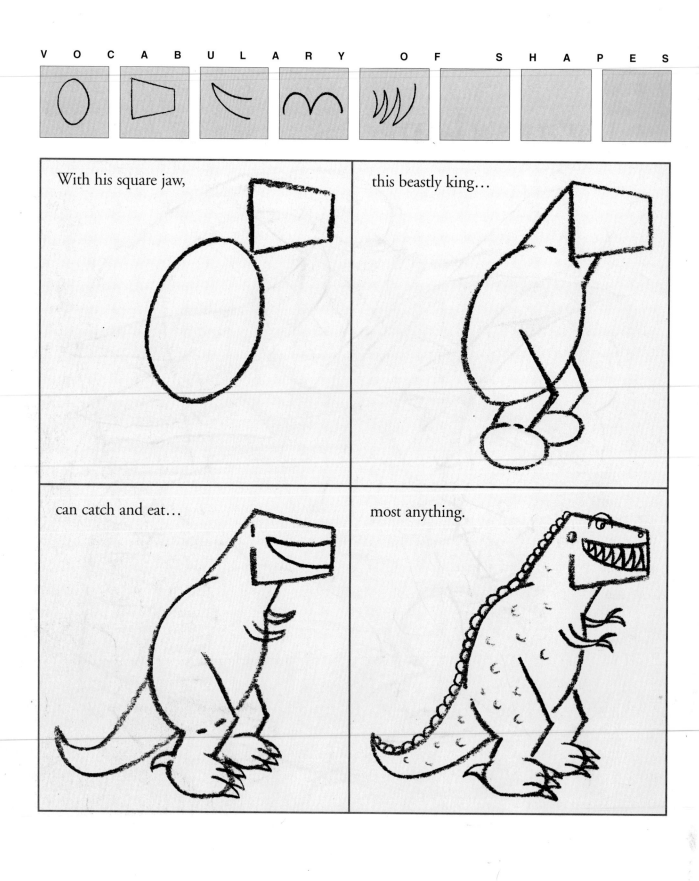

With his square jaw,

this beastly king…

can catch and eat…

most anything.

Tyrannosaurus Rex

On his back...

is a diamond wall,

but his brain...

is very small.

Stegosaurus

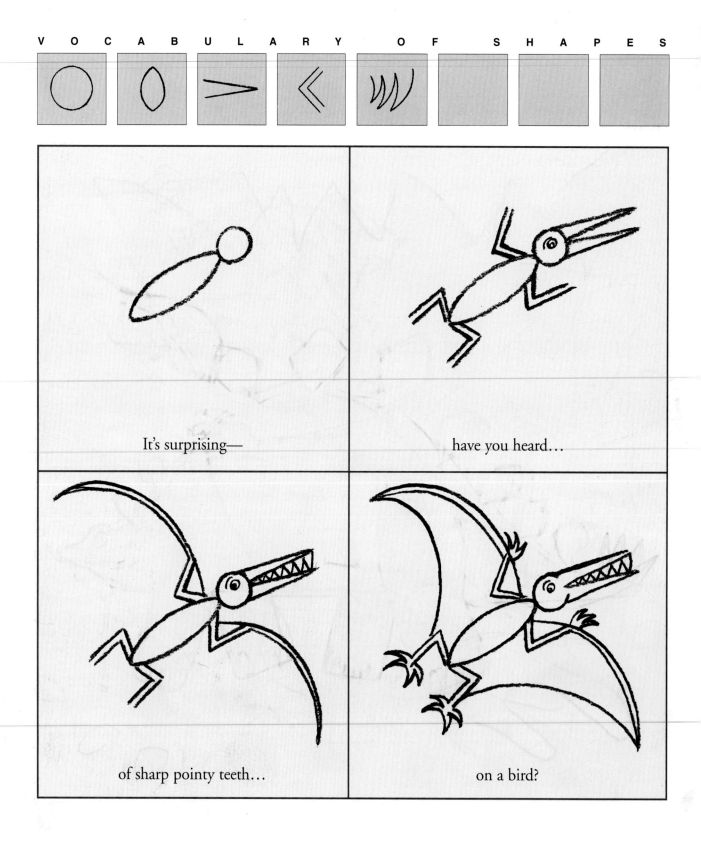

It's surprising—

have you heard...

of sharp pointy teeth...

on a bird?

Pterodactyl

With triangles covering…

her back and flank,

She looks just like…

an armored tank.

Ankylosaurus

Even though the dinosaurs are extinct,

you can recreate each one with colored inks.